SOME GOOD WRIT

Christmas, Cancer, Dad, Wine, Sex and Jeff

JEFFREY BAILEY

Table of Contents

"Take It Back"

Moon on darkness

Stately it sits as if to whisper

An ungranted wish

A blemish on the face of black

Never is there any turning back...

Navel-gazing expanses

Blur the lines

Between what we want,

what we get, and

what we project.

Lying down in sweet repose

My window's never completely closed so everyone knows

Streaming dreams in the cinema of the muted night

May affect and resound with the masses...

Tomorrow I'll never have to worry-

I'll never had to take it back.

"Demagogue"

We're waiting on an anti-Christ.
In the land of the free, the home of the brave
You thought some of us didn't deserve the benefit of being new
but that's how you won this race.

Decades of political correctness run amok and not put in check;
sometimes we react viscerally
before we think things through thoroughly..

but those external stimuli
which once would have made you happy
to see us cry
are now our violent reactions
against years of torment from the likes of you which belie
my fear of being a victim so you can be heard
because of your feeling alienated just as I was for years.

Your fury, your furor, your leader
Your fetishes put you in his cult
but depending on how you conform blindfolded
and if you swallow
you could be exalted when Jekyll, Hyde and their puppeteer
are all in agreement your praises must be sung
because until the strings come loose
he wants you under his thumb.

"Empathic Collapse"

When the ones who see the signs have senseless reactions

logic renders intuition an exercise in self-derision

to our prying eyes looking for wisdom.

The channel surf is a practice of discernment

as our fortunes rely on the fortunes of those

whom we trust

will not flip

on a whim.

When our prophets unrehearsed come to us through their stream of
consciousness

 as the prophets fall short from sadness

nothing will be reversed.

The astral travel of people hurt

projecting energy on their spoils

as if none of it were transmuted -

in anger "for entertainment purposes only"

they have the final word.

"Manna From Heaven"

More and more it comes to me
as Manna from heaven was sent
To Earth to consult
She said "Son if you're unhappy
   it's not my responsibility because you're an adult."

Just as Manna from heaven is supernatural
   My mother's instinct maternal:
   an illogical execution of a year-in-year-out
   post-partum ritual

"Just like Manna from heaven I will find a
job the way
just as Manna from heaven

I kicked your stomach on that Paris subway."

Something inside you thought there was
something wrong.

As Manna from Heaven I came through you
Only to have nothing and have this repeat
itself in nightmares liong-drawn.

Unlike Manna from Heaven

still can't figure out what my subconscious

can only tell me

  but as with Manna from Heaven

and as you said to me

  as an adolescent

"Dad and I don't know what life has in store."

Again, as with anything out of my

control,

I don't need you anymore.

"Words to Live and Die By"

There's something to be said for suffering

if only it's by choice;

to punish in advance

so you're not spoiled by riches

and can ensure success is in the offing..

And in a world unforgiving

with a destiny no matter how pedestrian

you can be certain there are lessons

that aren't blessings.

To avert failure by extraordinary means

align with each day's mysteries

as if to embrace the grace...

With the fire breathed as air

from the mouths of duplicitous faces

don't yield to all that's come to pass

as if that's that.

For in all achievement lies a balance

of torture and reward.

No one's gone beyond to live to tell

if penance righted a compulsion for avarice

or if the judge and jury rendered a guilty verdict

and threw down the gauntlet

on the whole world

when we all know we've hurt one another anyway.

Suddenly the notion of an afterlife

seems absurd.

"The Same Today"

I'm tired of adapting.

I can never be grounded

when all I'm doing is blowing in the wind.

Exploration was fine when I was in my youth

but all I was doing

was trying to find ways

to justify a childish attitude

never considering I was denying myself a future.

Where there have to be consequences

if there were no sacrifices

if but to maintain the same lifestyle

I had back then

meant I had to commit to something plain

I'd rather run away

and it's still the same today.

"Requiem for Aphasia"

Unless you're brain dead, the disaffected

all have excuses to be

and then

as is in system of entropy

 gibberish manifests within and varies.

 Instead of letting it degenerate

ask yourself what really led you

down a path of antipathy..

how you go down and not bring the rest of society?

If you're happy

 your missing a few screws

since there really is not much

about which to be upbeat

- whether it be our economy, whatever the screws'-loose anatomy..

try to get numb

you won't be the only one.

Scared of more change -

no matter.

You cannot resist fate

In stillness you move on passage's rite.

"Stagehand"

Played just as well as by any ingenue,
applause stifled by a low-rent warm-up artist
who never has to worry about climax;
each of hers being more penetrating than the last -
for her polish
best forgotten are his cues.

His jollies are ill-begotten -
mistaken that he runs the show;
just because on him too he wants the lights shown
that does not mean it's curtains with his say-so
or the inspiration will be afterglow.

Through his living vicariously
Through adolescents almost thirty years his junior
his bed's already made by his wife
who swallows her words as a captive audience
while all this Monday morning quarterbacking is absurd.

For the young girl, something came up short
but for everyone except her who came before, they knew of netherreaches
in the recesses of the shorn
from which some other girl's dream would be born.

"A Future?"

When your world takes a backwards spin

and when you've lost all footing

in the corner you've been put in

seldom does defeat seem as though

it's a new beginning.

Yet you try and try again;

it's as if to rise above

you keep on falling

because you've lost all sense of belonging.

The very thought of a future

not as promising as the past...

I'm afraid to leap from its precipice

and into all the trappings of its abyss

but some part of me

wants to relive it

for it was my only bliss

yet it only blurs the vision

of that life that could be something different.

What they took from me I will sorely miss...

The power to rise above

can only propel me to new heights

so that my star shines bright

to brandish the night sky from light years away

and blind them

to knock them off

the high-horses they ride

and regain my throne

their petty complexes convinced them they stole.

Too bad they're blinder than faith

because in time their own uncertain futures

they too will have to face.

God reserved these beautiful days for me

So the next time he unleashes storm fury

He let's me know your attempts to

Make me suffer

Are all in vain

"Hot Enough for Two"

The well has not run dry

but prevailing apathy is more regulatory

as life's demands are binding

and the right choices reap the fortune we've already known...

more risks than rewards –

When our lifeblood is supposed to afford us

life's creature comforts

yet we struggle against time

as responsibilities have to be abdicated

just to get by.

 The guarantee of your sanity is on the line.

You can be lead to practice chanting

in the scolding hot showers of morning mantras

intermittently breathing in and out

requisite ohms as the opening salvo

to screams in Sanskrit with intention to purify and center

as scalp spine neck arms shoulders

are the points of pressure

through which good prana will only come.

So you feel you must withstand

 this ritual of water torture

because the other part of you

cannot do all he needs to

lacking the will, discipline and pride to stand upright

besodden by the guilt of all the things the cannot undo.

Justifiably excused, what his ravaged soul and mind know he should do

but chooses not to

somehow rationalized by there not being water

hot enough for two.

"Certain Death"

It's all going to work itself out in the end.

That's just my fear:

I'm going to try to stand and fall...

when you're not here.

To know I'm right where I'm supposed to be

isn't always reassuring

when unsettling apprehension of what is to come

makes me question if I should just

turn tail and run.

Someday my own two feet

will be grounded long enough

to eliminate all doubt.

Whether upright on Earth

or at a horizontal haunt in a casket

I can be without the thought I was cursed..

or that each misfire and loss was through my own fault.

the bookend to this tale of woe

when I'm long forgotten

are their heavy memories which gnaw at them

of someone they wronged.

cut me a break
my mind's the only thing at stake
 the words we say are far from what we feel
 cut me a break
while i try to move the needle
 away friom what's real
holidays restrict

while you land there on a pillow...,.

trying to recoup any reserve of energy
 the smoke that billows from my chimney:
just more hot air coming from the house's mouth
that speaks in tongues about foreclosures on dreams
while its worried family prays to sleep
 just not to stay awake
 cut me a break.

preoccupied, wiling away precious moments
in the rat race where we're told
 to say grace
but there's not much more I can take
before we will all want to escape

 cut me a break.

"Loyal to a Fault"

My demons, the same as yours
possibilities too countless to let them weigh on us -
or yet to ignore.

Though too numerous,
they were considered calculated risks by others
who knew the prognosis
to be anything but propitious.

Loyal to you to a fault:
pacified you
allowed you to be immobilized by fear
and to be sucked in by until your insolence was quickly overwrought;

Pronouncements about stages of our decline from your doctor
whose bedside manner appear to be a bother.

Inured to this, he chose the profession
and yet he's the one the one more impassive.
We are defined
by the urgency to counteract aging with the wisdom of time
but the types of turmoil from which the chance of a future invites us to recoil
easily turning us away from the doctors' soullesness that render his insights
benign;

The missed appointments I knew you were too shamed

or humiliated to face:

showers were a balancing act;

too many pirouettes during which you had to bathe –

the final act

should have been to clean your asscrack.

The contours of the sidewalk bore out that your superstitions

 – although having run amok –

were heightened when

the wind tunnels pushed you back and drew an imaginary line

which rendered you more inert.

The path of least resistance was my loyalty to a fault;

only one day to find we never had the grit for pain.

We couldn't unwind;

the worst of it for you is upon us

yet all I about which I think in my anger as I lose you is

I was loyal to a fault.

All you want to do is be disassociative

closing your eyes, resigned praying for demise.

You fell and hit your head

more than just as if it were a wrinkle in time;

the ground's going to swallow us

but maybe the undertaker can wait to shift his unsteady hand

which has shaken us

times countless

but just maybe our fault lines

can straighten out

and beat time.

"Like a wife"

Her leave came to him as a shock -
 a man she stayed with
and seemingly could forgive.
And she sang his praises, "John's been my rock."

When you feel you've really made it through
and the years have cemented
what life has already fulfilled,
complacency is an unwanted foe
if for some reason unbeknownst to her
she can't let "it" go

she has to go
because a mid-life crisis means he gets his just desserts.

Like a wife, I was there.
Lying next to him on the floor, just to make sure he,
certainly not blameless, could make it all alone.

Like a wife, I took the derision
when he was trying to bar-hop
to escape a house-full of memories
that was our prison.

"Stop pouting"

"I'm not pouting"

Yes, you are - your moping so much your jaw is on the floor."

Then one night, he walked into my bedroom

from being alone at night

(this time as a lonely wife would) "I'm crying."

I said, "Yes, I know.

Oh my God", but it was my mother who dared to blast my life

eight years later,

"You're like a wife".

"HEY 19"

Resist tyranny

It's about that time to hunker down

But they'll whip you into a frenzy

Till you're so run down you can't get back up.

It's gone viral exponentially;

only you're not ready merely to be a specimen

n something so tragic

Would that to wear a mask would not seem over-reactive but pragmatic.

Resist tyranny -

it's at the point where the strength from our numbers

means nothing.

As we're barraged by dawning alarm

of fatalities which the teleprompters can never do justice

Spliced with a deadpan delivery from the innocuos fake blonde.

Resist tyranny -

She one of many wanting to shine

in a digital news paradigm

with that mousy voice flatly uttering

that the

"Dying are Multiplying."

Her incantation as all the others –
With no discernible gravity.

I wonder if she fears she too would get left behind
or is too vapid to think along the front line.

"Faces '22"

Thick-headed;

If of blood were the tears we shed

the saline that falls away

Is deceptively gray.

While all the faces eyes' penetrate

your shameful desire placates your sight:

inadvertently you cut your eyes to spite your face.

Embedded somewhere within the veins are contours;

they are maps of bloodlines to gifts;

when old wounds the bad seeds of which start to be absolved,

newer perfumes fresher and resplendent of lust

go unattended

by shorter shrift.

Words could never malign;

the journey to the cross has us walking six feet apart at a safe distance.

No one is talking behind your back accept the last man in the procession

presiding over the refrain

As he is unburdended by

the journey that plays again.

"What To Do"

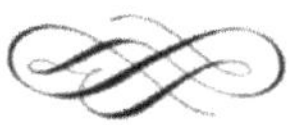

Hearing that voice again

that lets me

that tells me

I'm worthless,

 careless and I should

catastrophise

but...

Just to stop because I cannot self-actualize

would be juvenile

but would be even more so futile -

so I will persevere as long as I can...

with lies.

What to do when the cup runneth over?

What to do when the only path I saw

is the one that makes me steal

from what I realize now is a mere pittance

but I mistook for

resource so grand

to carve longterm passion and bliss??

The glamor of keeping cool

Justifies the sweat

Of having to be one step ahead of your doddering next.

I'm only able to pull off this feat

if we both can grow into these clown shoes

In which less is more and more is less –

with similitude to a past to which you

almost out of the need

the wanting out

didn't have to take even a

breath before intensely realizing

in the bat of an eye we had nothing left.

The passion is never be forced

if at all costs you can and will

rationalize its pull.

"RECLINE"

An imprint worn down by years

A figment, a shadow of oneself

Strained by the stain of blood,

sweat and years.

Crime scene outlines

a life that suffered merely one blow too many;

yet non-descript are the shadows which will never again project any body.

An autopsy's possibilities encompass a story less revelatory.

No time to rest on laurels

No time to reminisce

It's do AND die

To shy away and never take a risk;

rather to live a life sublime

Instead of one

Of an indifference past the point resigned.

In slumber for all time we recline.

"It Was Written"

She took my hand to write our story

She wanted her coffers filled

And unto me her first blackmail a mere ruse

implied threats to sell me down the river

All because of ill-begotten reviews.

It was written by the tension in my teens;

the repression of having to cover in front of someone else -

who was perpetrator

Of the abuse -

something else which I had to play off

as if I could never be part of the scene.

It was written all as though it were fly-by-night but always predictable;

as with you my adrenaline rushed

But there was no fight or flight response;

It was written I, the nerd spaz, could not fight back;

That's why at almost fifty-years I am,

as it is written,

susceptible to flushed adolescence:

When you win by the theft

Of my composure you see through my words

Which on a screen are to your disapproval and suddenly those words are bereft.

Not to say it is written I am your conquest;

If as imagination has revealed I can let my words out and put a new lease

on a life of weakness,

then maybe it is written

karma will eat away at you

As you write your life in reviews.

"Manmade Opposition"

Those who say

I take too much for granted

never live in His image

In the moment naked.

You never look at your reflection

or worry about what it should resemble

or worry what becomes of you

when it's all destined.

Opportunity has already been built;

the hand of fate strokes and caresses

while the hands of the clock

want to reign in my fun.

No I won't let man's

self-imposed opposition

define who I've become

before I've even begun.

Shame's ocean of drowning souls

living fast, dying young

while their tired spirits and minds unsung

somewhere next to nameless bodies like vessels

through which their lumber is carried are just beaten down enough to make them lose their way

mistaking the stressful passage of time

for a passion for life.

"BANKRUPT"

Remember our old ways
waking up in the afternoon
remember the marathon mayhem
we used to make.

We weren't the only ones running;
time was roaring fast
nothing much has changed-
people living a rat-race everywhere.
One day blends into the other
except you're not there.

You'd give as good as you'd get
It became a power-trip
by your own admission
You let the deposit slip.

A firm devotion to what I should have expected;
even if this were divinely deranged
for mutual benefit.

You wanted all the credit
but I thought you would never leave;
co-dependence
was our policy's guarantee.

Only one day you wanted to flee;
the day you took liberties
with what was love
was the day it all went away.

Wished you paid me an advance
to stay.
I can't bank on a second chance.

Morally bankrupt with nothing;
no pride as if it could be salvaged
no peace of mind
for a love unacknowledged
for you lady injustice so blind.

"Home All Along"

I fled a place

that brought shame to me

and was bigger than I

never facing the truth of what I should be.

Destiny's pushing me back

telling me to fix what I lacked

as if there were a second act

but who was to know this was home all along?

I don't deserve merely

a modicum of happiness.

I had that; it's fleeting.

If I have to stay here who would've known

for me

for me this would be home all along?

Time may cover the shame like a band-aid

but there's never any hiding

from the mistakes I've made.

That's how I know I've been short-changed.

Here I am trying to go forward

tabula rasa carte blanche;

the cynicism which has brought reservations

has led me to a flight-or-fight response

to leave the home I've known all along

with no reward hoping to stand on my own.

"Up"

Things are looking up every day

If only I keep my chin up

I'll be at level with my own head

which the naysayers say is in the clouds.

I sleep at work but I am not day-dreaming.

I am high

yes I'm high but only trying to run

on happiness as if it were fuel

but energy needs to refilled

I shouldn't need something renewable

if the fix is a love eternal.

"(Success)Relinquished at Birth"

No say in the matter

just as

so it goes

it does't matter you were born.

Shadowing embers..

from fire a symbol

primal;

if only you were born out of a need

for we're told to create

yet with no one but us to intercede.

Society's beat is to a machine.

The wanton indolence under the guise

of sin

isn't enough to deter

the resistance within.

When success is as elusive

as the powers-that-be are recklessly dismissive:

Light a fire under my ass

to motivate to fulfill

a need a thirst

so basic in its achievement

it shouldn't hur;

yet you take pleasure in the art of my masochism at work.

So it doesn't matter when

ultimately

you have no say in the matter.

The determinant of survival:

Success.

There's no in-between

not anything

other than a condition of circumstance

by the sleight of the hand of a superior power

on Earth as it is in Heaven

survival then death;

in the middle the road is paved

with ambition and a prayer

but maybe not

success.

"Surprise Tell"

In the devil's workshop

No overtime

Just know the limbo

that is his closing time...

It's his way of marking you

Full of dread

for what you may have said

that tomorrow could spell the end.

So freely sell your wears tonight

The emperor has no clothes..

I found my fallen angel –

the handsome devil himself

with a special kind of tell.

It will build character of the soul

To know in absence passion is foretold.

This morning in hopes of purity,

the company of orifices of last night's possibilities

are doubly holy.

The Capricorn I want me makes me mistress;

The burn of the cleanse

will make the grips on each other more intense.

We turned loose on each other

because he smacks of underground swag

and his love of his wealth on and in me is a succulent brag.

Fabricate any story, but the first time he went all the way down

with all eyes on us

that I wanted them all to cry.

I massaged the head while your tongue is fire

That breathes the power

into my snake

not in the Garden of Eden

but mine in our bed.

"No Pay, No Stay(More than Temporary)"

Let me be your example

You may think you exacted some kind of revenge

but more to the point I illustrated you're an asshole's sample

ripped you another for exerting a perverse pleasure

in holding in your hands

your team's unnecessary anxious wonder.

Let there be excuses

Of four weeks, you dropped two deuces

and perhaps insolvency for more expensive weeks ran too deep

so clutched were your purse-strings

that even former subjects can recall deficiency.

Venmo, Zelle, CashApp,

who is this third-party Sulay?

Is he the front to this, as the French would say, bidon operation?

What future favors he'll want from you will come back to bite you anyway.

On a holiday weekend

shut off the headphones and let Avaya ring.

My Dad's bag of bones laid up with pneumonia

but I'm weak from the blood that is my money I don't have at mid-day;

while out of spite you're refusing to see the glaring short-sidedness

that shouldn't amidst all my hardship

to you be an unprofessional blindside.

No pay, no stay

A visceral reaction to another one of your delays.

"Habitual Sabotage"

You've been here
but I've not been right all these years
You must have had the touch
but we lost it...

too long ago to know to remember
how it could mean
losing so much.

I can put down the drink
but cannot stop in sobriety
from saying the things I know are true
but don't want others to know I think.

I can't trust you forever
but there's no personal harmony
between that and never;

when we'll all come and go –
how we'll never know
what will be the way
not
to be swallowed whole.

"Unattainable"

Court your favor

when there is no one

or nothing else

that could ever compare

to the basic pleasure

you are able to give yourself

in response to a yearning so primal

yet for you and me is ephemeral.

Toys, dolls and wine...

machine operated notions of the already disdained time

dictating mechanical desire;

never to think this comes at the expense

 of so much to repent.

This too shall pass –

our desired end:

happiness.

To court your favor

when happiness is a notion

whose pursuit destroys its own advantage

only to find scars are badges not bandaged.

"Giving Up, Giving In"

Marching to the beat of my own drum

I've found very little reason to carry on;

following you for lack of anyone better

maybe this time I'll have direction

more incentive to get my life together…

Something always takes me out of a comfort zone.

It's as if I'm hiding from the unknown

whoever or whatever

a cover I didn't know I had

was blown…

These little blue pills still calm me down

(not a peep out of you)

but I'm feigning for something more

in unfortunate tolerance to a reality

I couldn't see before

when the dosage seemed as if it were more;

change was not merely out of necessity

but a cloak I wore.

I thought going with the flow

meant accepting the status quo

and not trying to hold on

to something so desperately

meant inevitably someday I could let go.

Now out of the abyss of apathy

the light is blind promise in purgatory

and there's an inured acceptance to the fact

I won't be able to adapt when all that's in front of me

sets me further back from happiness.

Nothing to show for the years

except a cynicism that perverts

whatever dreams I wanted to work

and instead brought tears.

"Life Will Paralyze"

"Life will Paralyze"

Why come out of the womb

And push

if life is in God

And in his hands all things good

I needn't anything

Not even a prayer if my life

When you tell me I should

If in time all his work is done

then you cannot deny that my time

waiting

is that faith divine so many urge me to have

But He derails me from what's mine

For if in his own light

he stands eternal and non-subject to the imposition of time

I guess I should accept he can make me wait till the judgement's end

And that he can never be reproached when I'm dead

"Why Feel Shame?"

"Why Feel Shame"?
You told lies when everyone expected
you to rise
and defy a pattern
set in motion so long ago.

It's hard to know
when the transgressions began
and if theirs ever underhanded were planned
out of retaliation against you
because your voice
somehow threatened them.

How much you must have sacrificed
through the most desperate of times
just to save some part of them
when they wanted to
project their own vices onto you.

Jesus dying on the cross for our sins
was the ultimate virtue
and they'd tell you so should you.

Why feel shame
when your aura supposedly cleansed

deceives your ability to reason

and you let this happen

over and over again?

Why feel shame

when orders come down

without their answering your questions?

Knowing how they'll belittle you

tells you they're making you the target

of a jerk-off peep-show

designed to control you.

Looking for the next opportunity?

Before you someone was doing the same

who would fall from grace

trying to hold on

leaving open for you your next vacancy of shame.

Born into a world

blanketed by the unknown;

looking for absolution in advance of all not foretold.

Maybe a baptism can unwind our lives

to a utopia unencumbered by the stigma of pain

and the self-inflicted persecution of shame.

"Anti-social Conditioning"

I bask in what you would term mediocrity;
the more leisure time the merrier.

I'll accept this place in life laid back and chill
not worried about the future
subdued by pills.

I'll let out a carefree me
albeit disgraced.

I shouldn't have to be proactive –
to plead for things I should have and need
while the rat race
endless anyway
begs you to increase the pace
just to live in a world
none of us chooses to embrace.

It's kind of hard to love yourself
when your identity is more than your name
when the only thing each of us has
are thoughts...
be they of our fleeting successes
or of our grandest failures
or what could have been –

or of our childhoods however bleak

which were the only periods of promise

with the worlds at our feet.

Come into this world with something to prove

and if it's a self-fulfilling and calculated goal

it passes muster for a calling

even if you're an ass@@le.

Even when God's lost souls

whom you deem pretenders

have to try harder

just to swallow their pride to get by

can't keep silent and suck it up

they have to let it go for good.

"RegressionAGGression"

Suppose to accept

all my limitations:

only experience is the intermediate illusion

when survival

the only solution.

Grasp at straws;

maybe you'll find

your life's calling –

all the while

still accepting

you've settled for less -

but you still must persist.

You've been brainwashed into thinking

all this is a blessing.

The realm where your spirit lies

and where success is monetized

don't always coincide.

Our natural state to be free – –

to hunt is to achieve;

so society's runaround

turns a man back into

his counterpart

neanderthal.

"Suspension of Divine Disbelief"

Oh God

my supposed savior

I've fallen to my knees again.

Don't even know if you're here

Just for the things

I need

to keep me alive;

your son gave it all up for all of us

but I must swallow my pride.

You gave me this life.

You knew what would become of me

before I had the option

to believe.

Blind faith's

the only prayer I have left.

Huddled up to you now

when I'd rather turn my back on you now.

I wonder what it would take

for either one of us

to pass as something

other than fake.

In your eyes

or those of the anti-christ

see that I never cross the lines

so that to this occasion

I may rise above creation.

"Formative: Peripatetic"

I spent the earlier days as peripatetic –
homeless, if you will – consider me a child who could never sit still.

Never put down roots to grow, I was
made of heartier stalk but brittle was my will.

If the bar is merely to adjust, just watch me
succeed by detachment apathetic;
another day to be mentally self-reliant
part of which implied my survival was silence
which nowadays is seen as characteristic
of one so violent.

The formative years came and went
but still a childhood foretold an adulthood
when for no cultivation of human or personal interests
would forever make a life's difference.

Thumb-sucking maybe through grade five,
carry this overbite for the rest of my life.
18: drank the wine;

No strides in passage or milestones achieved.
Mom says my mental age and memory deceive.
16, panic attacks

The doctor presented counciling
as a way back;

Instead Dad just threw out the referral;
only one in this family nuclear could be
whack...
even if a year later anxious in Chemistry

I felt I
would hurl
my legs would uncontrollably shake
because the subject matter on top of an already ridiculous workload would elude
my mastery.

14: years on Clonazepam
Everything filtered chilled
drawback: clammy withdrawl, make you
think of worst case scenarios.

You take action you can't take back
but at least you're cool as a cucumber
and happy as a clam.

"Generational Dysfunction"

Incorrigible dirigible,

more than able.

The jealousy weighs on me.

I'm clunky

my red cheeks on the outside

hide the hurt gnawing from clenching

from keeping from saying all I feel bound to do...

Is shovel it against the tide.

A chance encounter;

I've only been taken by my own promise -

a dream that makes me weak -

if only my constitution could have stood down the predatory thieves.

They did to me what I did to my father;

in this I am karma central

but I never have to see the scheisters

but as my eyes can no longer meet Dad's,

the mirror is now not my only potential captor

as my regret has the makings of familial disaster.

"Ornamental"

So crowded is our personal space

The creche once stately is no longer its full village;

just to walk by to see it apart at your feet is sacrilege.

The embroidered initialed stockings

laid opulently brimming on the floor;

The children in their growing wisdom

compare lists to see who courted best

the favor of the jolly old bastard

amidst the wrapping paper and string lights

that pose a fire hazard.

The tipping point when a tree becomes ostentatious:

what is merely chintzy

what is ornamental

falls under the weight of a hundreds-year-old pine

meant to carry

the perennially fragmented memories

of many a yuletide night.

The angel on top becomes victim of

its own flight;

there are many fallen ornamental bulbs – not nearly as much light.

As for the setting of the Christmas table,

put those side-by-side who complement each other;

their drunken banter may delight, but rapport should not devolve into their
becoming a blight.

A sense of decorum is a positive refrain –

even if peripheral guests while you're under the influence are still lame.

And, for those whose presence is so past benign,

the prospect of having to invite them back makes you drink before it's time.

So to the rest of you who may deeply slumber

I say," Goodnight to all and to all a good night."

"The Grinch's Lament"

'Twas all at once,

everything went haywire

not even a way to salvage Christmas

not even if The Grinch insists.

The boxes in the cellar with tangled lights;

our cat wants to climb the tree,

eat a poinsettia.

For once this year,it can drink the water from the toilet bowl;

not from the base of the tree.

The angel we set struggles to watch over tinder –

as if protection were not already

the largest part

of its annual agenda.

With the limits placed on generosity,

and no broad brush without which we paint,

we're forced into monochromatic oblivion –

the etiquette of gift-giving

sadly renders Christmas no longer quaint.

Generality "Happy Holidays": too generic.

Merry Christmas: too denominational.

The prospect of spreading cheer :dismal.

Maybe the outlook for gatherings

will be abyssmal.

"Rising Christmas Day"

Find the meaning

of Christmas time.

If you're pure of heart

as on any other day

it's the call to let your spirit waft –

so the hints that suggest clues about our innate gifts

outweigh the adrenalized promises

of what's in a box.

Santa anonymous

With humility and brisk pace

can't help but be among the last-minute shoppers;

as the saintly one suffers

in his occupation, he holds the reins...

globe-trotting on his sleigh,

he's left holding the bags of a world of merriment's abrupt end –

where the children would be mistaken in their chagrin about their letters unanswered

learning to accept it all as magic when it's pretend.

"Resolution(New Year's Eve)"

Finality for time's own sake;

Auld Lang Syne gives poetic license

to a one day mass exodus from a chronic hangover's absence.

To erase our errors

accelerated by a doomsday hourglass,

we set the illusion

that we can keep partying round the clock;

and what we resolve will soon by ritual

come to pass.

After the the promises of lives unfulfilled,

the human construct of time leaves its own behind.

A fleeting second of our lives can bring four numbers in a millennium to a streaming stop,

yet new patterns of human behavior

cannot be taught.

Not for a celebratory retrospective or revelry of deeds

does this party assuredly

favor excited screams

but the prophets who can be right or wrong but once

are perennially revered;

the citizenry cheers

as champagne flutes clink

a little before the dawn

the weak spells are tested

as soon as the alarm rings.

What are you doing this New Year's Eve?

"W.V.P Workplace Voodoo Priestess"

A voodoo priestess with an ax to grind

wants to speak through you

as if she were choreographing failure

through the seeds of doubt she planted

in every utterance

every stutter

found in the words you chose.

Court of public opinion favors her;

she's been exalted to her high horse

for she's the standard-bearer for the underclass

and she can more readily mold those unlike me.

Ward off the curses she possesses

by realizing she is frivolous

when what counts is your personal best -

whether in her proximity or far away from her

if I may be so lucky.

If she feels your efforts are uneven

or your passion inconsistent

maybe you can convince her otherwise

by blocking her out

through a persistence which will lead to success

and a courage which will never cease.

"No Good Pictures(A Click and A Shot)"

For our lives to be enhanced

but we're never ready for capture;

for us to feel significant through their prism of their lens

we continually commit narcissism.

We'll take a picture albeit prematurely

and a shot for posterity is one more click's posthumous lesson.

Anything to gussy yourself up

For the unrelenting sixty-seconds non-stop

If you're lucky,maybe it will be photoshop

or the app that can sharpen your eyes, unbloat your face

for no picture should show any kinds of mistakes.

Point and click

Your body will convey everything it longs for: approval even fame.

The perfect shot-

it clicks and pops, but no picture is enough

to portray you for the star power you've got.

When you feel no pictures can do you justice,

through habit and despair you take another one;

while that shoot's not done, another one has begun

and its director has chosen to cast randoms -

yet with his training he only has to be right once.

Possessed by the limelight, he claims his work is,
as any selfie would attest ,a whitewash, a cleanse
something to reassert his confidence.

"The Fight for Life"

All I've created doesn't seem as if it is much

if you believe all you are

could be gone by the divine whim

of his touch.

Blown away by life's vicissitudes,

no one was more guarded than I

to have floated by the skin of my teeth

so casually for so long

until all their words went in one ear

and out the other

but I was not going to let their indifference put me asunder.

So their not knowing what side of the fence I was on

by their own reasoning made me wrong.

The resistance I met

only made me stubborn

but don't fault me

when I could've been consumed by regret.

You can't expect others to understand

who you are if the only force which directs you

is by someone else's hand.

Some ask, "Why push on?"

Some ask, "What's the sense in being strong?"

If only to face this outcome all along?

The fight for life isn't in vain to stay alive;

it's your having the belief in yourself against those who told you

you couldn't achieve those dreams

and that you would

have to suck up your pride

to fight for your life.

The fight for a life won

which defies the odds

I'm never complacent, never resting on my laurels;

but by my own will is when it shall be done.

The fight for life

has no morals imposed;

it won't punish for secrets and lies told

where in this domain

I never chose to toil.

"Refuse: A Noun and A Verb"

For as long as I can remember

I've had to take my glasses off

before walking by a mirror.

I may not have wanted to check myself out

but I sure felt it was no accident

 because if we refuse to look into ourselves

then we cannot have the refuse leave doubt.

When what's inside never was addressed,

I could not look back and below long enough.

it may have been dark and warning red -

yet I was intentionally aware of the danger it meant.

I was as blind as justice with its eyes wide open -

in the dark to something

from which I wanted to hide

but if but for fear the scales were not tipped in my favor,

I thought I knew better than to know.

Movement rarely cohesive

dribs and drabs here and there

the age requirement has been lowered to 45, if you care;

splotching somewhere on a circular chair...

Inadvertently catching a glimpse

when somewhere a fallen angel had to bring it to light

the litmus test told a fortune of fright

but my eyes were strained from age so I, male , menstruated against the tide.

At greater risk because of a family history,

obese and having drunk irrevocably,

at risk for ulcers and pollups;

as those before me I stand in the throes of a towering shadow

that casts a long pall over me.

Better "man-up" as I delay my colonoscopy.

"Never Knew"

So many reasons to be afraid -

I think I just about gave up

until you came.

A leap of faith and beyond is what it takes

to make a victim stay.

Never knew love without conflagration;

it's a new flame with the promise of pain;

pray this

doesn't blow up in my face.

Of the greatest passions I've known,

there's a thin line between love and hate.

Never knew you would let me down

until you saw me as unreasonable

when all I wanted to do

was to turn this...

into something real.

Another lover is all you will be.

If the substance of your words

could match just one moment of our time together

love would be fertile verdant ground

away from the quagmire of your lies.

Never knew I could fall
with a precedent set;
that I could never know a love so strong -
if it were only in your arms I belonged.

Never knew why you were so resistant;
never knew a feeling so unrequited
all of it leading
to your leaving tonight.

"Underachievers"

They gave you days to weeks

but if to you life was always pain

even with the flesh-and-blood one you claimed

to love by your side,

it was never really a matter of time.

You lasted less than a week to the day.

I misguidedly tried to be the hero for both of us.

So it didn't matter if I gave up

or if your laziness

or how fast the wind blew

or if my saying I slept too poorly to take you

makes me a liar;

I didn't know where your shortcomings started

and mine with yours blended;

neither of our gifts complemented the other's

because we would still take them for granted

even if we were both still alive.

If all we did was butt heads

and for all pleasantries before;

your last words to me were "You bastard".

Encepalopathy of the brain took the reins

while as the end of the story grew nearer

the doctors said,"There was no reading between the lines.

"You are going to die"

Haunting memories of you drugged out as if you were a feign

out on a sidewalk adjacent to our former apartment on Main Street;

for the longer I wanted you to hold on, it was I who

in fewer than a two-day home hospice

administered prescribed doses of morphine

to relax the heart so you wouldn't suffer needlessly;

the last one I withheld in hopes in you there would not be enough

but the final say was not mine - God felt the lack thereof was just right.

By this time, your fight to survive did not require you to be of sound mind

so I'll never know if you knew it was me you left behind.

Obstructing my ability to will you to live

when our problems will now and forever

yield no solutions -

but two underachievers are better than one.

Riddle me this:

three hospitalizations in the course of six months,

two urinary tract infections

one bout with pneumonia

two rehabs -

how many doctors and tests

how they could have missed all this?

If those were the right places at the right time

then on the night before his second-to-last release yet stay of execution,

my layman's position that something else was making him worse,

my demanding a CT and bloodwork was all it took,

but it was too late

but all these underachivers have nothing on me:

the one who most hurts.

"Enmity/Entity"

There's really no right way

when we all walk among one another clear as day

through a world where either you or I

can turn on a dime.

Maybe the refuge we seek in the dark of night

keeps the shadows of paranoia at bay

so our own motives won't come to light

since the truth's so elusive we'll never find it...

but within our own power

where fear is impervious to reason

still we can't vanquish

those who would hurt us with a sneer.

Can't draw lines in the sand

against those we're not sure are friends;

loving only one's self is the gesture

to preclude all of this conjecture.

If too much is censored

even from perceived adversaries

and no one is free to question

when the expansion of civilization requires an imagination

then without passion

free spirits will incubate

until their gestation renders them mercenaries.

The future however mechanized
as the present is bereft of surprise;
still we take one another for granted
as we hide behind devices in what's left of time.

Looking for meaning in an accident,
looking for an ounce of compassion;
committing atrocities to arouse suspicion
against a faceless enemy
in a subjective reality
to gauge if he's innocent or guilty.

Random acts of kindness
televised as a bookend to horrific evening news stories;
Big Brother's hypocrisy: a blessing in color
when in such disorder there is no black and white
while all the oppressors get all the glory.

The pangs of urgency galvanize the insecure
while the faceless entity endures.

"Not Just a Phase"

This really is the place it all began;
everything's off course and I'm off-kilter again.
This time I'm fighting;
it's anyone's guess
why I choose to be alive.

I'll be damned if I'm going to let
them determine
my sermon or epitaph;
the world seems intent on
my having involuntary
mishaps.

In the moment I tried to ignore
their stares and laughs as if it were a contagion
those laughs I enjoyed from a safe distance
rendered me complacent not aware this incubation
through my own gaffs
would be the catalyst...

I could never turn back.
I'm still trying to stay afloat
when all that's left of me is the demon
who won't be exorcised –
just to endure as an amorphous being
that yet again won't define me.

"Awoken"

Since indifference became sin
You should have just left me alone
You go your merry way, I'll go mine...

Not everyone here can find meaning
in their lives...
Still I keep pace to a rhythm with no rhyme.

Instincts which lie to us
inhibit us from realizing that something
greater inside...

We never can be too careful
when dreams are underwhelmed
by a reality you can't comprehend
let alone awoken actualize.

"When I Knew You Before"

So much in a hurry to get home

the boy inside will never grow

not even yet a man but he understands;

it's all the same as being alone.

When I knew you before

can't pinpoint precisely when

the resignation began...

When I knew you before

I was the calm before the storm.

When I should have been relieved

in spite of all I've seen,

the ground continually

pulled from underneath me.

When I knew you before

when I should be looking forward

as your beacon as your son

Somehow I've lived it all down

in more ways than one.

"A System's Failure"

Deep beneath the cracks in your armor

lies a soul where buried self- admissions were reading as a scroll:

a map to an ultimate destiny that left for us no time to be calmer

yet for all the shame that turned into cancer,

you still left me with more questions than answers.

Deferred to me on all the decisions you refused to make

so when I took liberties with your own words and wishes

you remained obstinately defiant

when to me to keep you alive

was not a hard decision at which to arrive.

The biopsy was a no-go.

The doctors said you had days to weeks;

You were deemed too stubborn tor chemo.

The goal was to make you as comfortable as possible.

In the palms of our hands

where our curled fingers merged,

I already knew after speaking to your rehab roomie

there was more at play than had yet to be learned

when you were coughing red loogies.

Hospitalized three times in the last six months,

and no one thought to look more closely inside his distended hernia once.

To be so insidiously stealthy as not to show itself before stage four,
exonerating doctors who try to talk people into sharing
their own innocent oblivion,
while my Dad's physical history excuses the inexcusable system thirty-five years
on
from the abject failures of a system deemed wonderful
in the malpractice courts of second public opinion.

No feeding tubes, no ventilators –
to me those were the "extraordinary measures"
you did not want taken.
When you thought I wasn't looking, I heard you say,
"I just want to die".

Still, I wonder when you said that
if you were in your right mind
or thought I wasn't there
so somehow it would be easier
to take the path of least resistance...
and leave me behind.

Your father, my grandfather of pancreatic

There's no sense being contrarian and arguing:
First they'll do nothing
before risking doing any harm;
Lack of action, a violation of the Oath Hypocratic.

Your sister, my aunt of ovarian

the family tree's

rotted terminally.

"Utilitarian Truth"

There is no such thing as utilitarian truth.

Throw stones at the realist.

He who tries to impart it

He who deigns to speak it: the leverage is his hubris.

He is shunned as an elitist.

It dawns not with morning; it is as fleeting as the fundamentals on which it is supposedly built.

It takes the form of words only;

we exist "in theory"- that is why it hurts.

You are loath to practice something You have not done first.

"Embarrassment"

Woke to my judgement day as though

it were to someone else's delight;

without an acolyte,

 the power they had was an illusion

I was not going to put up a fight.

Ambition, initiative;

the former seems too grandiose

while the latter humbles you

to where you're supposed to have no semblance of pride

 and you'll take whatever is proposed

because inside you at the highest strength of convictions

there is something immeasurably priceless

about having some place to call home and hide.

Still I wear an unwavering embarrassment

even if I no longer toil

in the gutter of your shadow

wondering about my tomorrow.

"Left Behind(Post Mortem)"

The way you went out left nothing to be desired

I couldn't put myself in your shoes -

or you in mine;

the negligence of time

left us both behind.

You were out of your mind

asking what time I arrived in town

to which I replied,"twenty years ago and so did you."

If only you could see through my eyes,

you'd know it all snuck up on us

as if we were abandoned but responsible

for having been left behind

missing all the signs.

The orderly unwittingly fighting with you to take your pills.

I backed them up

but ultimately there was no battle of wills, you couldn't swallow;

it killed.

Liberties with interpretation of your wishes

 when you told the doctors it was me to whom to defer;

anything was still met with your defiance proxy.

I could not even have peace of mind

just to get you to have a biopsy.

Maybe while you ignored my pain

you could only focus on yours;

maybe you talked yourself into the idea 71 was "dying of old-age material";

if in all plausible denial you thought you could shield us,

with the little time you left behind, the diagnosis would never be official...

Except the problem with that is it is two months later

which feel as though it were two years

and in your grave per your wishes

are your ashes you never thought to scatter.

I guess bucking tradition meant writing this addendum

thinking of the money you would save;

funny how you had a plot all along

for which you thought you had completely paid

but what was of you left behind thanks to the crematorium

we'll never be able to ask about post-mortem.

"In Retrospect(The Die Was Cast)"

Vengeance against the ignorant among us

pointlessly it festers in dreams

infiltrates the light

as I only want to revise history to make me right

Waking up to the dawn

brings it all back;

would that I were a different child

would that I were certain of a conviction -

maybe then I could only resent myself

instead of feeling attacked as an adult by everyone else.

Yet my doubts should be erased

a bully's in jail

and still the pitch of paranoia from one's hand smacking the back of my head

was the stuff that made school bus rides

until eleventh grade intolerable..

in retrospect even more now than then.

Amplified by peers' innate ignorance -

that alone should have prevented me

from rumination for all these years.

To have taken their words seriously was my mistake in retrospect;

soon rejected then detached,

my parents were too oblivious when the die was cast

to inquire why I no longer deliver

what they had come to expect.

Just as their assertions about me were a surprise

when they thought I wasn't looking,

as they glibly uttered them

 I await in stoic repose

 as we all grew older

 and became more alone

as their projections came to reveal more about them

as frightening as t was for a child

in retrospect all manner of deficiency was shown.

I never hit back

and going back I wish I could have done more than that

there are no apologies

but what I did in time

right to the end

you both gave in promises

that fell flat.,,

just as Dad did when his die was cast.

"The Host Character(The Other Side)"

Dared me to turn to the other side;

not to turn away...

but the reflection I saw

I didn't recognize

be it of course not by choice.

I've been wearing in my denial

many a disguise.

At all costs

I never wanted to look at them;

as if what lied on the other side

peered back at me

shattering some illusion

I'd awaken from a fantasy....

Conscious effort not to feel

Mask the wonder not to value

all that's real...

Knew I had to heal

but wasn't about to

let memories of the past

steal moments

if for just some moment
I'm in the clear.

I was an apathetic soul.
Through ambivalence of thought
The past, the present...

the future
won't knock on my door.

But instead of letting go
I stepped outside
letting myself go...
hung myself with just enough rope
losing all control.

"Illusory"

Prophecies I do live by

take to heart all the things

when you paved the way...

Even if dreams don't come true

I can't shoot the messenger

it never came from your mouth

your Word is Gospel

and you are a fallen angel

a minion who somehow sent a sign

I should spite you.

I am tired of faith

guilt me into feeling obliged

wile away the hours

I live by the clock

Times flies and it will be all done...

My time will come...

but you knew it wasn't in the cards

I am what I am today

The love of many but too few

Could make up for you.

Cascade down a rainbow
to a pot of gold
I follow you blindly
just goes to show
how to stumble into a spectrum of fortune all at once
but it cannot bring rewards that bring eternal returns
because the light at the tunnel is not
The Way to the other side.

www.ingramcontent.com/pod-product-compliance
Lightning Source LLC
Chambersburg PA
CBHW040154160726
48006CB00014B/1747